Reading & Writing *Excellence*

KEYS TO STANDARDS-BASED ASSESSMENT

STECK-VAUGHN
BERRENT

A Harcourt Company

www.steck-vaughn.com

ACKNOWLEDGMENTS

Project Author: Kathleen Fitzgibbon

Executive Editor: Carol Traynor

Senior Editor: Amy Losi

Editor II: Caren Churchbuilder

Editor I: Edward Nasello

Associate Editor: Christy Yaros

Assistant to the Editorial Dept: Virginia Giustino

Project Consultant: Howard Berrent

Art Director: Frank Bruno

Design and Production: Susan Geer Associates, Inc.

Designer I: Julene Mays

Design Associate: Gregory Silverman

Cover Design: S. Michelle Wiggins

Photo Research: Sarah Fraser

Illustrators: Elaine Garvin

Yuri Salzman

Lynn Titleman

Steck-Vaughn/Berrent is indebted to the following for permission to use material in this book:

page 96   "Bella Had a New Umbrella" from BLACKBERRY INK by Eve Merriam (Morrow Jr./HarperCollins). Copyright ©1985 Eve Merriam. Used by permission of Marian Reiner.

Photo Credits:
Cover ©Gettyone/Grant V. Fair, p.32 ©Peter J. Bryant/Biological Photo Service; p.50 ©Gerard Lacz/Animals Animals; p.51a ©Milkins, C. OSF/Animals Animals; p.51b ©Zig Leszczynski/Animals Animals; p.82 ©2001 Gavin Fine Art & Design.

STECK-VAUGHN BERRENT
A Harcourt Company

www.steck-vaughn.com

ISBN 0-7398-3951-9

Copyright © 2002 Steck-Vaughn Company

Published by Steck-Vaughn/Berrent Publications, a division of Steck-Vaughn Company.

3 4 5 6 7 8 9   TPO   06 05 04 03

Table of Contents

Students are instructed to approach a selection and test question using the
Four *R*s: **R**eady, **R**ead, **R**espond, **R**eview.

Unit 1 introduces multiple-choice and short-answer questions, using
the three levels of comprehension—literal, interpretive, and critical.
This unit focuses on specific strategies designed to assist students in
answering multiple-choice and short-answer questions.

Unit 2 explains how students can use graphic organizers to help them
answer essay questions. A graphic organizer accompanies each of
three selections. Students are given instruction in how to use the
different organizers to answer essay questions about the selections.

Unit 3 builds on what was taught in the previous two units.
Students apply what they have learned to answer multiple-choice
and open-ended questions about various selections. There are hints
to help them answer each question.

Unit 4 provides students with an opportunity to independently
practice the strategies they have learned. This unit may be used as a
test to assess students' learning and to simulate formal tests.

To the Teacher

Reading & Writing Excellence is a series of instructional books designed to prepare students to take standardized reading tests. It introduces the **Four R s,** a strategy that will enable students to read selections, understand what they have read, and answer multiple-choice and open-ended questions about the reading material. Special emphasis is given to using graphic organizers as prewriting aids for answering essay questions.

Many genres, such as fiction, nonfiction, poems, fables, and folk tales, are included. Some of the passages are taken from published, authentic literature, reflecting the type of instruction that exists in classrooms today. The questions accompanying each passage represent the different levels of comprehension.

The material in this book provides your students with step-by-step instruction that will maximize their reading success in classroom work as well as in testing situations.

The Four *R*s to Success

People follow plans every day. Plans help you. Plans give you steps to follow.

Think of a reading test. A plan will help you understand a story. A plan will help you answer questions about the story.

Here is a good plan to follow when you take a reading test. It is called the **Four *R*s: R**eady, **R**ead, **R**espond, **R**eview.

Ready   Before you read, you need to get ready.

► **Think about why you are reading**   Are you reading to answer questions for a test? You will be looking for information. You will also be reading to understand the story.

► **Look at the story before you read it**   Read the title. Look at the pictures. Guess what the story will be about.

Read   The next step is to read the story.

► **Picture what you are reading**   Ask yourself, "What will happen next?" As you read, guess what the next part of the story will be about.

► **Check your guesses** Think about your guesses as you read. Are things turning out the way you thought they would? Keep making new guesses.

Respond Now you are ready to answer the questions.

► **Read the question** Read each question carefully. If there are choices, read them carefully.

► **Think about the question** Which parts of the story will help you figure out the answer? Read those parts again. If you have to write an answer, think about what you want to say before you write.

► **Answer the question** You are now ready to answer. If you have choices, more than one answer may sound right. Choose the BEST answer. If you write your answer, state your ideas clearly.

Review Always review your work.

► **Check your answer** Look at your answer. If you have choices, make sure that you picked the best choice. If you wrote your answer, make sure that you answered the question completely.

Types of Questions

Multiple-Choice Questions

A multiple-choice question has more than one answer choice. You must read all of the choices. Then choose the best answer.

Here is what a multiple-choice question looks like:

The word <u>nap</u> means

    Ⓐ to run.

    Ⓑ to sleep.

    Ⓒ to sit.

Short-Answer Questions

A short-answer question does not give you any choices. You have to come up with the answer on your own. There are lines to write your answer on. You will write a few words on the lines.

Here is what a short-answer question looks like:

What did the dog do before it took a nap?

_____

_____

PART A

Multiple-Choice Questions

Follow these steps:

STEP 1 Read the question carefully. Then read all three answer choices carefully.

STEP 2 Think about all of the choices. Look at each choice. See if it makes sense. Look back at the story. Read the parts that help you answer the question. Choose the answer that makes the most sense.

STEP 3 Mark the best answer. Mark your answer correctly. Find the bubble next to the best answer. Fill in the bubble completely.

Practice Multiple-Choice Questions

Mark your answers correctly.

Fill in the bubble beside the best answer choice.

Do **not** use a check mark. Fill in the bubble completely.

Do **not** mark an "X." Fill in the bubble completely.

Do **not** fill in part of the bubble. Fill in the bubble completely.

This is correct. Fill in the bubble completely.

Try It!

Which animal has four legs?

Ⓐ   Ⓑ   Ⓒ

DIRECTIONS: Read this story about a boy stuck in traffic. Then answer questions 1 through 4.

Stuck in Traffic

1 Mom pulled the car onto the highway. Traffic stopped. Blake asked if they could listen to the music station. Mom said, "No." She needed the radio tuned to the traffic report. Nina opened her eyes wide and tried to stay <u>awake</u>. She didn't want to mess up her hair. She liked to look good at junior high. Blake looked out the window. He felt bored.

2 Yesterday at school, Ms. Ling called Blake aside. She said, "Blake, I enjoyed reading your story. Let's put your story in the school newspaper." Blake thought about Ms. Ling's words. He smiled. He looked out the window.

3   Finally, the car stopped in front of the school. Blake looked at the car clock. One half hour to get to school! He had better rush to class!

4   In class, Ms. Ling said that they were going to play a game. They were going to tell a group story. First, Ms. Ling told about a cat and a mouse. Then, Blake added three sentences to the story. Next, Amber added to the story. Then, Tran continued the story. The story was funny. Blake laughed. He couldn't wait until it was his turn again.

5   The next morning, Blake got in the car. He fastened his seat belt. Nina looked sleepy. Blake looked out the window.

6   Then, Blake had an idea. He knew a fun game the family could play. This game would help pass the time while they were stuck in traffic.

DIRECTIONS: Read each question carefully. Fill in the bubble next to the best answer.

1   Who played the story game right after Blake?

Ⓐ Amber

Ⓑ Tran

Ⓒ Ms. Ling

STEP 1   Read the question carefully. Then read all three answer choices carefully.

STEP 2   Think about all of the choices. How are they different? They are names of different people in the story.

Look back at the story. Read Paragraph 4. Look for an *order word*. Order words tell you when things happened. Here are some order words: **first, next,** and **last.** Who played the game **next,** after Blake? Find the person's name.

Now choose the answer that matches what you read in Paragraph 4. This answer makes the most sense.

STEP 3   Now mark the best answer. Find the bubble next to the best answer. Fill in the bubble completely.

2   Why did Ms. Ling want to put Blake's story in the school newspaper?

Ⓐ   Ms. Ling heard Blake laugh at the group story.

Ⓑ   Ms. Ling thought Blake wrote a good story.

Ⓒ   Ms. Ling likes stories about cats and mice.

STEP 1   Read the question carefully. Then read all three answer choices carefully.

STEP 2   Think about all of the choices. Look back at the story. Read Paragraph 2. Look at the words Ms. Ling said. Find the reason she wanted to put the story in the paper.

Now choose the answer that matches what you read. Make sure your answer makes the most sense.

STEP 3   Now mark the best answer. Find the bubble next to the best answer. Fill in the bubble completely.

3 The story says "Nina opened her eyes wide and tried to stay <u>awake</u>." What word means the OPPOSITE of <u>awake</u>?

Ⓐ open-eyed

Ⓑ asleep

Ⓒ away

STEP 1 Read the question carefully. Then read all three answer choices carefully.

STEP 2 Read the sentence for clues to find the meaning of awake. What is Nina doing to stay awake? Then, think of what the opposite meaning would be.

Which word tells the opposite action of staying awake?

STEP 3 Now mark the best answer. Find the bubble next to the best answer. Fill in the bubble completely.

4 Look at the end of the story. What do you think Blake did next?

Ⓐ He played the storytelling game with his family.

Ⓑ He looked out the window like he did every day.

Ⓒ He listened to the music station on the radio.

STEP 1 Read the question carefully. Then read all three answer choices carefully.

STEP 2 Think about all of the choices. Look back at the story. Read Paragraph 6. What game does Blake know?

Which sentence above tells about Blake's idea to pass the time? Choose the answer that makes the most sense.

STEP 3 Now mark the best answer. Find the bubble next to the best answer. Fill in the bubble completely.

PART B

Short-Answer Questions

Follow these steps:

STEP 1 Read the question carefully.

STEP 2 Think about what the answer might be. Look back at the story. Find clues or information to help you answer the question.

STEP 3 Write your answer on the lines. You will write a few words. Reread the question to make sure your answer makes sense. Check your spelling and handwriting to make sure your answer is clear.

Practice Short-Answer Questions

Write your complete answer on the lines below.

Be sure to

► Follow the directions carefully.

► Spell correctly.

Try It!

What is your favorite sport?

_____

_____

DIRECTIONS: Read this story about the legend of the dream catcher. Then answer questions 1 through 4.

The Legend of the Dream Catcher

Based on a Lakota Sioux Story

1   A spider was quietly spinning her web. The web was above the bed of grandmother Nokomis.

2   Each day, Nokomis sat and watched the spider work. Slowly the spider added to the web.

3   One day, Nokomis's grandson came into her room. "Nokomis! Watch out!" he shouted. He took off his shoe and walked near the spider. He held the shoe up in the air.

4   "No," Nokomis said. "Don't hurt the spider."

5   "Why do you protect the spider?" asked the boy.

6 Nokomis smiled, but did not answer. When the boy left, the spider went to the woman and thanked her for saving her life.

7 "For many days you have watched me spin my web," said the spider. "You liked my work. You saved my life. In return, I will give you a gift."

8 That night, the moon shone on the web. The spider said, "As you sleep, the web will catch your bad dreams. Only good dreams will go through the small hole in the middle. My web is my gift to you. Sleep well."

9 Today, people make dream catchers from yarn. The dream catchers are made in the shape of spider webs. People hang them over their beds to catch bad dreams.

DIRECTIONS: Read each question carefully. Write your answer on the lines.

1   Nokomis liked to watch the spider work. What was the spider making?

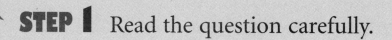

_____

_____

STEP 1 Read the question carefully.

STEP 2 Think about what you read. Look back at the story. Reread Paragraphs 1 and 2.

Look for the parts that tell what the spider was making. Think about the best answer.

STEP 3 Reread the question. Write one or two words for your answer on the lines. Make sure your answer is clear.

2   How are a dream catcher and the spider's
web the same?

_____

_____

_____

_____

STEP 1   Read the question carefully.

STEP 2   Think about what you read. Remember that only the last paragraph talked about dream catchers. Look back at the story. Reread Paragraphs 8 and 9.

Think about how the two are the same. The main clue is in Paragraph 8.

STEP 3   Reread the question. Write your answer on the lines. Remember to answer only the question. Check your spelling and handwriting.

3 Nokomis's grandson took off his shoe.
What was he going to do?

_____

_____

_____

_____

STEP 1 Read the question carefully.

STEP 2 Think about what you read. Look back at Paragraph 3.

Why did Nokomis's grandson call her name? Think about why he would take off his shoe. Then read Paragraph 4.

STEP 3 Think about the best way to answer. Write your answer on the lines. Make sure your writing is neat.

4   What was the spider's gift to Nokomis?

_____

_____

> **STEP 1** Read the question carefully.
>
> **STEP 2** Think about what you read. Look back at Paragraph 8.
>
> Read what the spider says. You will find the answer in this paragraph. Think about what the question asks.
>
> **STEP 3** Read the question again. Write one or two words for your answer on the lines. Make sure your handwriting is neat and your answer is spelled correctly.

Summary

You have learned how to answer two types of questions.

Multiple-Choice Questions

Mark the best answer.

Short-Answer Questions

Write your answer on the lines.

Remember to follow the **Four *R*s** plan below.

Ready—**Get ready to read**

► Think about why you are reading

► Look at the story before you read it

Read—**Read the story**

► Picture what you are reading

► Check your guesses

Respond—**Answer the question**

► Read the question

► Think about the question

► Answer the question

Review—**Check your answer**

Graphic Organizers:

The Key to Answering Essay Questions

The Essay Question

In Unit 1 you answered multiple-choice and short-answer questions. Another type of test question is an essay question.

Get Organized!

It is easier to find something in a neat drawer than in a messy drawer. Just like a neat drawer, it is easier to answer an essay question if you are organized. You organize ideas before you write.

A **graphic organizer** is a picture. It helps you put your ideas in order. First, fill in the graphic organizer. Then, use it to answer the essay question.

In this unit, you will learn how to use three kinds of graphic organizers: a **Story Train, Venn Diagram,** and **Character Web**.

Practice Essay Questions

Follow these steps:

STEP 1   Read the story and the question carefully.

STEP 2   Fill in the graphic organizer. Look back at the story. Find clues or information to help you complete the graphic organizer.

STEP 3   Use the information in the graphic organizer to write your answer. Be sure to do the following:

► Follow the directions carefully.

► Tell what you are writing about in the first sentence.

► Start each sentence with a capital letter.

► End each sentence with a period, exclamation point, or question mark.

► Spell correctly.

DIRECTIONS: Read the following story about a boy's first day at school. Then you will use a Story Train. It will help you write about Michael's morning.

The First Day of School

1 I'll never forget my first day of school. How could so many things go wrong?

2 First, I overslept. I don't know how it happened. The night before, Mom helped me set the alarm for 7:00. I had a hard time falling asleep. I thought about my new teacher. I wondered what kind of work we'd do in second grade.

3 Then, I woke up and looked at the clock. It read 7:30! I jumped out of bed. I ran to the bathroom. On the way, I hit my toe on the corner of my toy chest. It hurt!

4 Mom came in. "We're late, Michael! What are you doing on the floor?" She bent over and checked my toe. "It will be okay," she said.

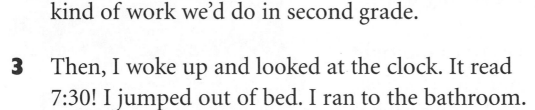

5   My toe hurt too much to have a shoe on it. I looked at my new black shoes. I couldn't wear a new shoe on my sore foot. So, I put on one new shoe and one sandal.

6   At last, we arrived at school. I caught my shirt on the car door. When the door closed, my shirt was caught in the door! Mom helped me get my shirt out of the door, but it ripped.

7   I walked up to the school. I was wearing one shoe and one sandal. I had a hole in my shirt. I was late! Mom and I stepped in the classroom. I didn't see my friends.

8   "Hello," the teacher said. "Welcome to first grade!" I was in the wrong room!

9   Finally, we got to the right classroom. I told my class about what happened that morning. Everyone laughed, including me. After that, the day got better!

Story Train

A **Story Train** helps you put things in the order they happened. Look at the **Story Train** below.

Michael sleeps late. He hurts his toe. He must wear one new shoe and one sandal.

Beginning

Middle

End

A **Story Train** is made up of train cars. Write what happens at the beginning of your story in the train engine. Write what happens in the middle of the story in the middle car. Write what happens at the end of the story in the end car. The end car is the caboose.

Fill in the **Story Train** on the next page. First, read the essay question on page 30. Then, follow the steps on page 31.

Essay Question: Write about Michael's morning. Put the things that happen to him in order.

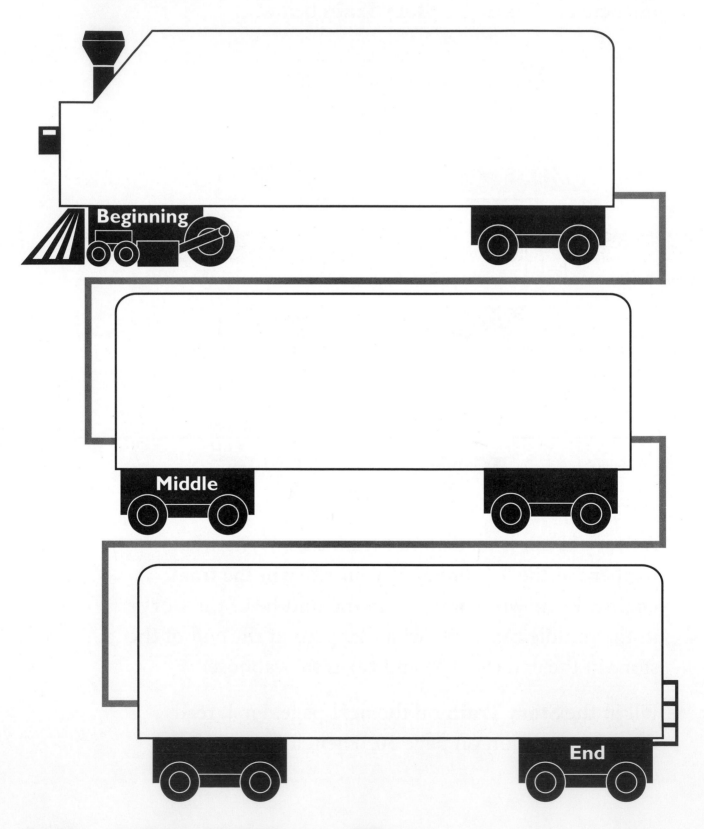

1. Write what happens first in the story in the train engine. Look back at Paragraphs 2, 3, 4, and 5.

2. Write what happens second in the story in the middle car. Look back at Paragraph 6.

3. In the caboose, write what happens last to Michael. Look back at Paragraphs 7, 8, and 9.

Now you have filled in a **Story Train.** Use it to answer the essay question on page 30.

Write down what happened to Michael. Write the things that happened in order from first to last. Write your answer on a separate sheet of paper.

Don't forget the fourth **R** in the **Four Rs: Review**. Make sure that your writing is the best it can be. Use the checklist on page 110 to help you.

Speak Out

Read your essay aloud to your class. Use your voice to make the story exciting.

The California State Butterfly

1   The next time you see a butterfly, look closely at it. Are the wings black and yellow? Do you see a shape that looks like a dog's face? If you do, you have found the California state insect. It is the dogface butterfly.

2   Only the male has the dog face shape. The female has yellow wings. She has one black spot on each wing. The male and female wings look the same on the bottom. The bottom is yellow or green.

3   The male and female are the same size. Their wings are about two inches across. You can find these butterflies in California. They are in the mountains. They are also in the hills and forests.

4   The next time you see a butterfly, look at its wings. Do you see a dog's face?

Venn Diagram

A **Venn Diagram** helps you show how two things are alike and how they are different. Look at the **Venn Diagram** below.

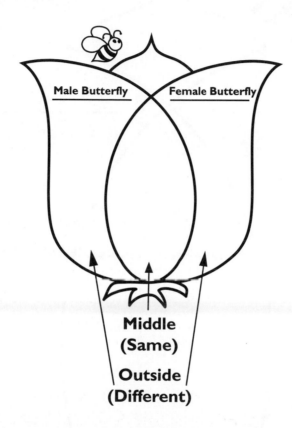

A **Venn Diagram** has two parts. They cross in the middle. You can see these parts in the flower above. The name of the first thing being compared goes at the top of the left part. The name of the second thing being compared goes in the right part. The things that are different are written in the **outside** parts of the flower. The things that are alike are written in the **middle** part.

Fill in the **Venn Diagram** on the next page. First, read the essay question on page 34. Then, follow the steps on page 35.

Essay Question: How are the male and female dogface butterflies alike? Use words from the story in your answer.

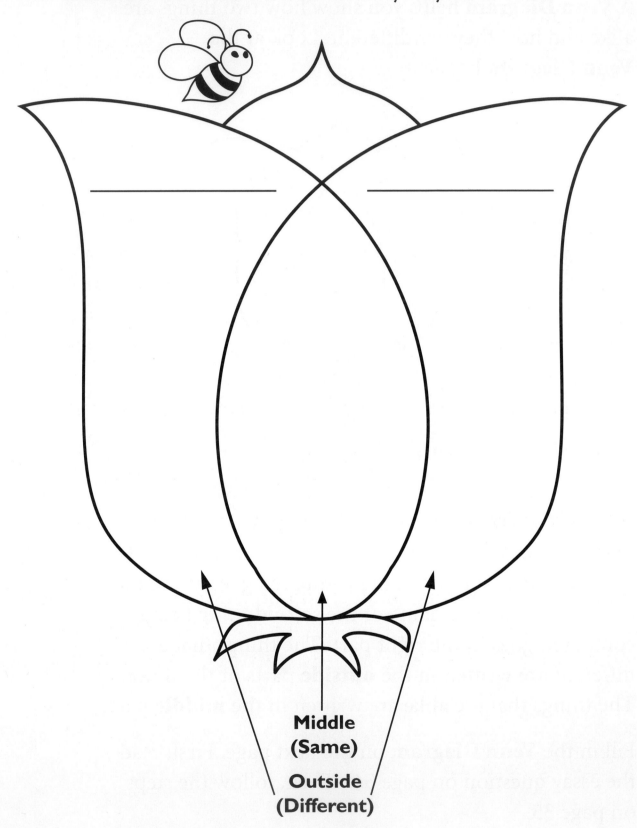

**Middle
(Same)**

**Outside
(Different)**

1. On the line at the top of the left part, write **Male Butterfly.** On the line at the top of the right part, write **Female Butterfly.**

2. Look at Paragraph 2 on page 32. How does the male butterfly look different from the female? Write your answer in the left part, labeled **Male Butterfly.**

3. Now look at Paragraph 2 again. How does the female butterfly look different? Write your answer in the right part, labeled **Female Butterfly.**

4. Now think about how the male and female butterflies are alike. Look back at Paragraphs 2 and 3. Write how they are alike in the middle part of the flower.

Now you have filled in a **Venn Diagram.** Use it to answer the essay question on page 34.

Use what you wrote in the middle part of the **Venn Diagram.** This is what is alike about the male and female butterflies. Write your answer on a separate sheet of paper.

 Remember to **Review.** Use the checklist on page 110 to help you.

DIRECTIONS: Read the following poem about a sleepy boy. Then you will use a Character Web. It will help you describe this boy.

Little Boy Blue

Little Boy Blue, come blow your horn,

The sheep's in the meadow, the cow's in the corn.

Where is the boy who looks after the sheep?

He's under a haystack, fast asleep.

Will you wake him? No, not I,

For if I do, he's sure to cry.

Character Web

A **Character Web** helps you think about what a character (or person) from a story is like. Look at the **Character Web** below.

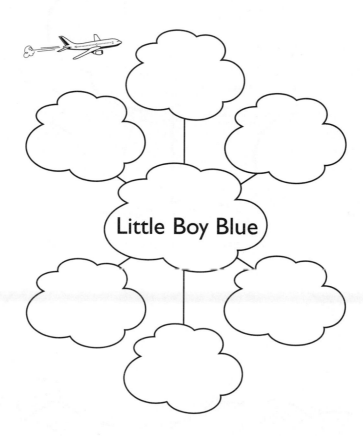

This **Character Web** is made of clouds. The name of the character goes in the middle cloud. Smaller clouds go around the middle cloud. Words that describe the character go in the smaller clouds.

Fill in the **Character Web** on the next page. First, read the essay question on page 38. Then, follow the steps on page 39.

Essay Question: Describe Little Boy Blue.

1. Write the character's name in the middle cloud. The character's name is **Little Boy Blue.**

2. Next, read the poem for clues that tell you about Little Boy Blue. Find words that describe the boy. Write the words in the smaller clouds around the boy's name. You can write one or two words in each cloud.

3. Fill in as many clouds as you need. You do not have to fill in all of the smaller clouds.

Now you have filled in a **Character Web.** Use it to answer the essay question on page 38.

Look at the words you wrote in the clouds of the **Character Web.** Use these words to describe Little Boy Blue. Write your answer on a separate sheet of paper.

 Don't forget to **Review.** When you are done, make sure that your writing is the best it can be. Use the checklist on page 110 to help you review.

Summary

You can use graphic organizers to help you remember what you read.

Graphic organizers help you answer essay questions. They help you put your ideas in order before you write your answer.

You have learned about the following graphic organizers:

 ## Story Train

 ## Venn Diagram

 ## Character Web

 Remember to always use the **Four *R*s:** **R**eady, **R**ead, **R**espond, **R**eview.

Guided Practice

Now you are going to practice what you have learned by reading some stories and poems. You will be asked to answer three kinds of questions.

► **Multiple-Choice Questions**—Read all of the choices. Choose the best answer.

► **Short-Answer Questions**—You have to think of an answer on your own. You will write one or a few words on the lines.

► **Essay Questions**—Use a graphic organizer to get organized. Then, write your answer. You can write a few sentences or a story.

You will be given a hint to help you answer each question.

Always follow the **Four *R*s:**

4Rs

Ready—Get ready to read

Read—Read the story

Respond—Answer the question

Review—Check your answer

DIRECTIONS: Read this story about a dinosaur looking for a change. Then answer questions 1 through 6.

Stuck in a Rut

1   DeDe the Dinosaur yawned and stretched. She walked over to the trees and <u>munched</u> leaves. DeDe said, "I'm stuck in a rut. Every day when I wake up, I yawn, stretch, and eat leaves. I nap. I yawn. I stretch. I eat more leaves. Every day is the same. I am stuck in a rut."

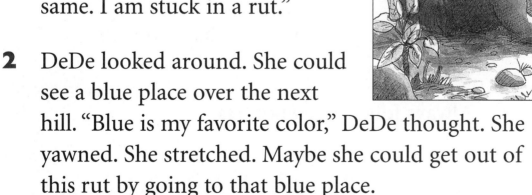

2   DeDe looked around. She could see a blue place over the next hill. "Blue is my favorite color," DeDe thought. She yawned. She stretched. Maybe she could get out of this rut by going to that blue place.

3   DeDe packed her bag and started walking. At noon, she found a tree she liked. She ate some leaves. She lay under the tree and took a nap. Then she sat up, yawned, and stretched. She ate a few leaves. She picked up her bag and walked some more. DeDe did this for three days.

4 On the third day, she lifted her head high into the air. What did she smell? It was a new smell. It was salty and wet. She saw the blue place in front of her. DeDe started running.

5 She stopped in front of the blue place. She stepped one foot in. It was cool. It was wet. It tickled her feet. DeDe watched a big white bird catch a fish out of the blue place! The bird flew over to her.

6 "Hi," the bird said. "My name is Peggy. I'm a pelican. Welcome to the big, blue sea."

7 "Every day is different here," said Peggy. "Sometimes it is hot. The sand burns your feet. Sometimes the waves are small. Sometimes the waves are big. You will find many new animals to play with here. Wait until you meet Terry the Turtle!"

8 DeDe sat in the shade of a palm tree. Today she didn't nap. She didn't yawn. She didn't stretch. She was in her new blue home!

DIRECTIONS: Read each question carefully. Fill in the bubble next to the best answer or write your answer on the lines.

1   Who is the story MOSTLY about?

   Ⓐ DeDe

   Ⓑ Peggy

   Ⓒ Terry

Hint   Look back at the story. Think about who is in every part of the story.

2   What caused DeDe to head in the direction of the blue place?

   Ⓐ Peggy told her about it.

   Ⓑ She had been there before.

   Ⓒ Blue was her favorite color.

Hint   Reread Paragraph 2. You will find the answer here.

3 What do you think DeDe will do next?

Ⓐ She will make new friends at the sea.

Ⓑ She will nap, yawn, and stretch.

Ⓒ She will go looking for a
new place.

Hint Think about how DeDe felt at the end of the story. Reread Paragraphs 7 and 8.

4 You can tell that <u>munched</u> means

Ⓐ sniffed.

Ⓑ chewed.

Ⓒ pulled.

Hint Reread Paragraph 1. Look for clues that tell you what DeDe did with the leaves.

5   What is DeDe's problem in the story?

_____

_____

_____

_____

Hint   Think about why DeDe wanted to go to a new place. Read the title of the story. Then reread Paragraph 1.

Essay Question: Write a letter to your friend. Describe DeDe the Dinosaur in your letter.

Hint   You will use a **Character Web** to answer this essay question.

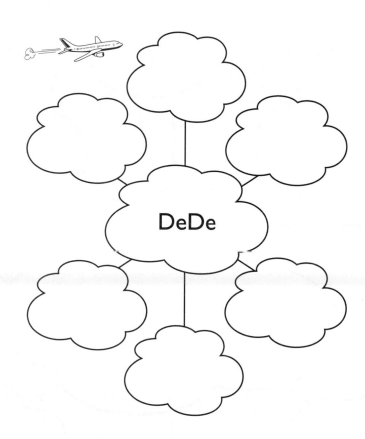

Remember that a **Character Web** helps you list things about a character. It has a large cloud in the middle. Write the character's name in the middle cloud. The smaller clouds are for words that describe the character.

Fill in the **Character Web** on the next page. Follow the steps on page 49.

Fill in the **Character Web** below to help you describe DeDe.

1. Write the character's name in the middle cloud. You will find her name in Paragraph 1.

2. Reread the story. Look for clues about DeDe. For example, DeDe sleeps a lot in the story. **Sleepy** is a word you could use to describe DeDe.

3. Write words that describe DeDe. Write one or a few words in each smaller cloud. You do not have to fill in every cloud.

Now you have filled in the **Character Web.** Use it to answer the essay question below. Write your letter on a separate sheet of paper.

6 Write a letter to your friend. Describe DeDe the Dinosaur in your letter.

Use information from the **Character Web** you just filled in. What things did you learn about DeDe? Use the words in the clouds to describe her.

Speak Out

Think about the blue place that DeDe went to. Write a few sentences that describe this blue place. Share what you wrote with your class.

DIRECTIONS: Many people have pets. Read this story about some animals who make cute and playful pets. Then answer questions 7 through 12.

Hamsters, Rats, and Guinea Pigs

1 What pet is fun to play with and doesn't need a lot of space? Some <u>rodents</u> make good pets. A rodent is a small, furry animal. It has sharp front teeth for biting. Here are three rodents that make good pets:

Hamsters

2 Hamsters sleep during the day. They are awake at night. That makes them a good <u>pet</u> for people who are at school or work all day.

3 Hamsters need a cage to live in. They need bedding in the bottom of the cage. They need to have the bedding changed once a week. They also need food and water every day.

4 Hamsters don't get along with other hamsters. It is best to keep just one in a cage. Hamsters may bite until they get to know you.

5 Pet hamsters live for one to two years.

Rats

6 Rats are very smart. They like to live with other rats. They need to be taken out of their cages and played with. They need to play for an hour every day.

7 Rats need to have their bedding changed once a week. They need food and water every day.

8 Pet rats live about two years.

Guinea Pigs

9 Guinea pigs are friendly. They also need a cage. Guinea pigs need to have their bedding changed every day. They need to get out of their cages to play every day. Guinea pigs are messy eaters. They need food and clean water every day.

10 Guinea pigs like to live and play with other guinea pigs.

11 Pet guinea pigs live for five to seven years.

DIRECTIONS: Read each question carefully. Fill in the bubble next to the best answer or write your answer on the lines.

7 What information would you find under the **Rats** heading?

(A) Rats live about two years.

(B) Guinea pigs are friendly.

(C) Hamsters sleep during the day.

Hint Look at the heading. Which answer choice is about the same animal as the heading?

8 What does the word <u>rodents</u> mean in the story?

(A) Small, furry animals with sharp front teeth

(B) Small pets that sleep during the day

(C) Friendly animals that live in a cage

Hint Reread Paragraph 1. You will find the answer there.

9 Why would you read this story?

(A) To learn about different rodents

(B) To find out how much a pet costs

(C) To learn how to make bedding

Hint Think about why the author wrote the story.

10 Read this sentence.

That makes them a good <u>pet</u> for people who are at school or work all day.

What does the word <u>pet</u> mean in this sentence?

(A) A teacher's favorite student

(B) To pat an animal gently

(C) A tame animal that lives with people

Hint The word <u>pet</u> has different meanings. Read the sentence carefully. Which answer choice makes sense?

11   How often should you change the bedding in a guinea pig's cage?

_____

_____

_____

_____

Hint   Reread Paragraph 9 under the **Guinea Pig** heading. Read the part about bedding.

Essay Question: How are hamsters and rats alike? How are they different?

Hint You will use a **Venn Diagram** to answer this essay question.

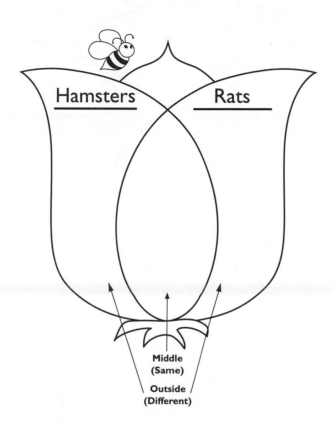

Remember that a **Venn Diagram** helps you see how two things are alike and how they are different. It has two parts that cross in the middle. The first thing being compared goes in the left part. The second thing being compared goes in the right part.

The things that are different go in the **outside** parts. The things that are the same go in the **middle** part.

Fill in the **Venn Diagram** on the next page. Follow the steps on page 57.

Fill in the **Venn Diagram** below to help you compare
hamsters and rats. You will write how they are alike and
how they are different.

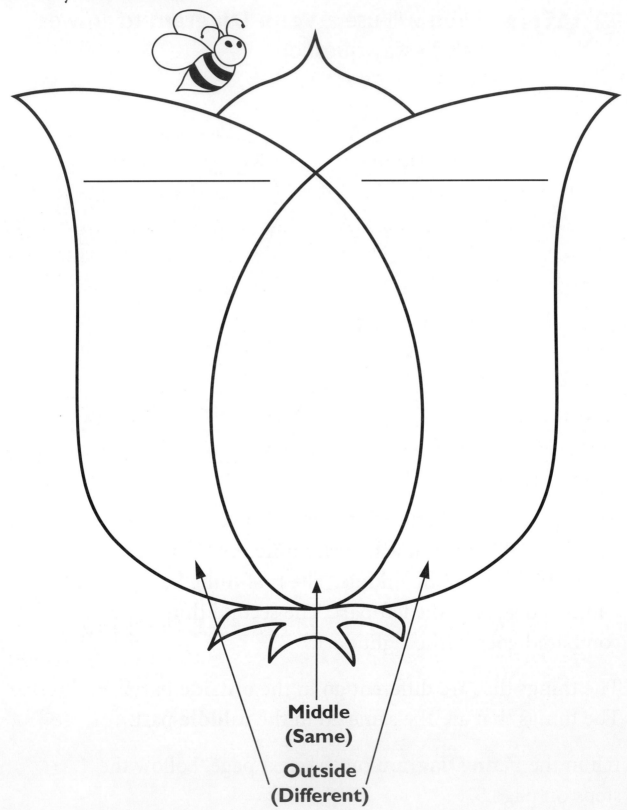

Middle
(Same)

Outside
(Different)

1. On the line at the top of the left part, write **Hamsters.** On the line at the top of the right part, write **Rats.**

2. Look at the parts of the story about hamsters and rats. What is different about hamsters? Write what is different in the left part, labeled **Hamsters.**

3. Now look to see what is different about rats. Write what is different in the right part, labeled **Rats.**

4. Now think about how hamsters and rats are alike. Write what is alike about hamsters and rats in the middle part of the diagram.

Now you have filled in the **Venn Diagram.** Use it to answer the essay question below. Write your answer on a separate sheet of paper.

12 How are hamsters and rats alike? How are they different?

Look at what you wrote in the **Venn Diagram.** Look at the **outside** parts to see how hamsters and rats are DIFFERENT. Look at the **middle** part of the diagram to see how hamsters and rats are ALIKE.

DIRECTIONS: Read this story about growing grapes. Then answer questions 13 through 18.

Growing Grapes

1 Four years ago we started growing grapes. Today, we will finally pick the grapes.

2 First, we had to dig holes. I helped my dad dig a big hole. "We need a big hole so the roots can spread out," Dad said. "A big hole with lots of room makes the grape plant happy."

3 We dug and dug. When the hole was the right size, Dad put one plant in. He spread the roots out and covered them with soil.

4 Next, we let the grapes grow. As the <u>grapevines</u> grew, they wrapped around a wooden pole we put in the ground.

5 Then, we cut the vines back. This is called pruning. Dad said we will get more grapes if we prune the plant. The vines grew long after we <u>pruned</u> them. I helped Dad tie them to the pole.

6 Finally, now it was time to pick the grapes. I picked and picked grapes. I set each bunch carefully in a basket. I did not want to squash them. I asked what we could do with all these grapes.

7 "Let's make grape jam!" said Dad. "We can have it on toast for breakfast. We can put it on a peanut butter sandwich for lunch."

8 We both laughed as we picked the last grapes off the vine. We couldn't wait to start making jam!

DIRECTIONS: Read each question carefully. Fill in the bubble next to the best answer or write your answer on the lines.

13 How long did it take the girl and her dad to grow grapes?

Ⓐ A few days

Ⓑ One month

Ⓒ Four years

Hint Reread the beginning of the story.

14 In Paragraph 5, what does the word <u>pruned</u> mean?

Ⓐ dug

Ⓑ cut

Ⓒ picked

Hint Find the sentence in Paragraph 5. Read the sentences around it for clues.

15 Where does this story take place?

Ⓐ At the beach

Ⓑ In a corn field

Ⓒ In a country garden

Hint Think about the title. Where does the story happen? Look at the pictures.

16 You can tell that the word <u>grapevine</u> means

Ⓐ a plant that grows grapes.

Ⓑ the skin of a grape.

Ⓒ the seed of a grape.

Hint Look at Paragraph 4. Use the little words in the compound word to tell the word's meaning.

17 What does Dad want to put on a peanut butter sandwich for lunch?

_____

_____

_____

_____

Hint Reread the words Dad said at the end of the story.

Essay Question: Explain how the girl and her dad grow grapes.

Hint You will use a **Story Train** to answer this essay question.

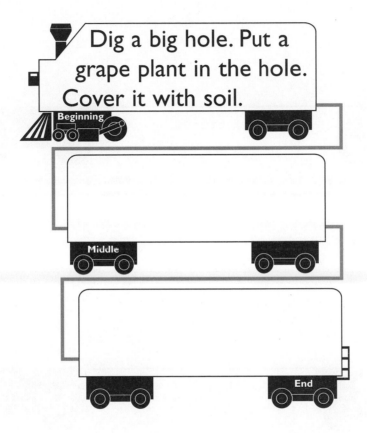

Dig a big hole. Put a grape plant in the hole. Cover it with soil.

Beginning

Middle

End

Remember that a **Story Train** helps you put things in the order they happened. It is made up of train cars. Write what happens in the beginning of the story in the engine. Write what happens in the middle of the story in the middle car. Then, write what happens last in the caboose.

Fill in the **Story Train** on the next page. Follow the steps on page 65.

Fill in the **Story Train** below to explain how the girl and her dad grow grapes.

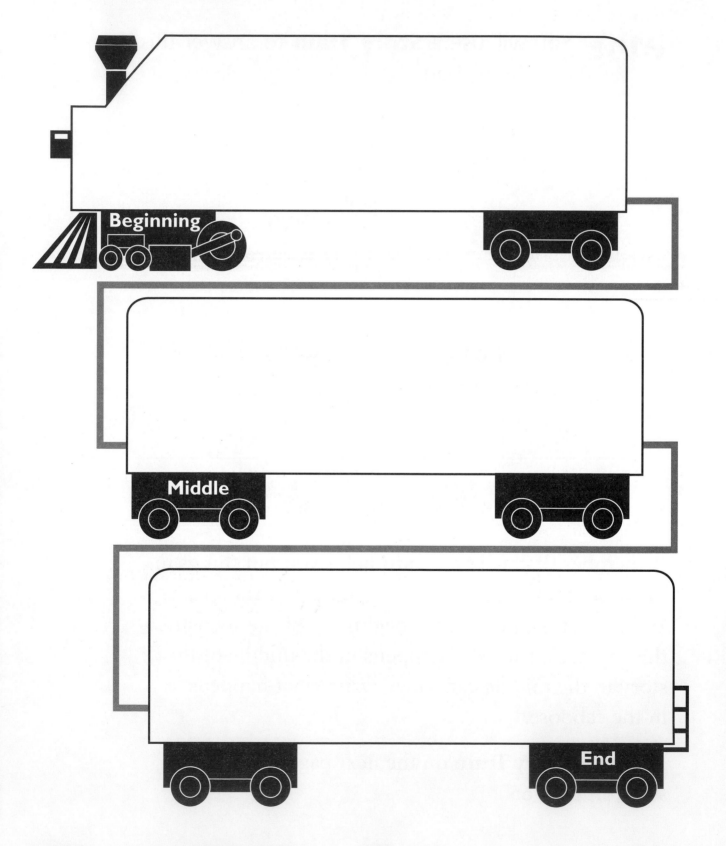

1. Write the first step to growing grapes in the train engine. Look at Paragraphs 1, 2, and 3.

2. What is the next step? Look back at the story. Reread Paragraphs 4 and 5. What does the girl do with her dad while the grapes are growing? Write this in the middle car.

3. What is the last step to planting grapes? Look back at Paragraph 6. Write this in the caboose.

Now you have filled in the **Story Train.** Use it to answer the essay question below. Write your answer on a separate sheet of paper.

18 Explain how the girl and her dad grow grapes.

 Look at the information you wrote in the **Story Train.** Write your story in the same order. Use the order words **first, next,** and **last** in your story.

DIRECTIONS: Read this poem about a kind of winter weather. Then answer questions 19 through 24.

Snowflakes

1   Merry little snowflakes

2   Falling through the air,

3   Resting on the steeple

4   And the tall trees everywhere,

5   Covering roofs and fences,

6   **Capping** every post,   **capping** = laying on top of

7   Covering the hillside

8   Where we like to **coast**.   **coast** = go sledding

9 Merry little snowflakes

10 Do their very best

11 To make a soft, white blanket

12 So buds and flowers may rest.

13 But when the bright spring sunshine

14 Says it's come to stay,

15 Those merry little snowflakes

16 Quickly run away.

DIRECTIONS: Read each question carefully. Fill in the bubble next to the best answer or write your answer on the lines.

19 What word in Line 8 rhymes with the last word in Line 6?

(A) coast

(B) where

(C) best

Hint Use the line numbers to find the two lines in the question. Then, look at the last word in each line.

20 What words in Line 4 have the same beginning sound as the first two words in "Twinkle, Twinkle Little Star"?

(A) "and the"

(B) "tall trees"

(C) "air" and "everywhere"

Hint Think about the sound at the beginning of the word <u>twinkle</u>. Then, reread Line 4.

21 What happens in the bright spring sunshine?

  Ⓐ The snowflakes cover steeples.

  Ⓑ Children coast on sleds in the snow.

  Ⓒ The snow melts.

Hint Think about what quickly runs away in Line 16.

22 Based on the poem, which word means the same as <u>sledding</u>?

  Ⓐ capping

  Ⓑ coasting

  Ⓒ failing

Hint Look at the words in the poem that have definitions. They are in boxes.

23 How does the speaker feel about snowflakes?

_____

_____

_____

_____

Hint Think about the kinds of words the speaker chose to describe snowflakes. Use feeling words, such as **happy, sad,** or **scary** in your answer.

Essay Question: Describe the snowflakes in this poem.

Hint You will use a **Character Web** to answer this essay question.

You have already used a **Character Web.** Now you will use it to describe the snowflakes in this poem. You will write words from the poem that describe the snowflakes. Write the words in the smaller clouds.

Fill in the **Character Web** on the next page. Follow the steps on page 73.

Fill in the **Character Web** below to describe the snowflakes.

1. Write what the poem is about in the middle cloud. Look at the title of the poem for a hint.

2. Reread the poem. Look for words that describe the snowflakes. What are the snowflakes doing in the poem?

3. Write words from the poem that tell about snowflakes in the smaller clouds.

Now you have filled in the **Character Web.** Use it to answer the essay question below. Write your answer on a separate sheet of paper.

24　Describe the snowflakes in this poem.

 Look at the words you wrote in the **Character Web.** Use the words to write what the poem is about.

Speak Out

Think about where this poem takes place. Look through the poem for clues. Tell your class where the poem takes place.

Summary

In this unit, you have practiced answering three types of questions.

Multiple-Choice Questions

Mark the best answer.

Short-Answer Questions

Write your answer on the lines.

Essay Questions

Fill in a graphic organizer. Use the graphic organizer to help you answer the essay question.

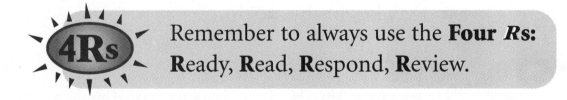

Remember to always use the **Four *R*s:** **R**eady, **R**ead, **R**espond, **R**eview.

Test

You will now take a practice test. Follow the directions. You will see three kinds of questions.

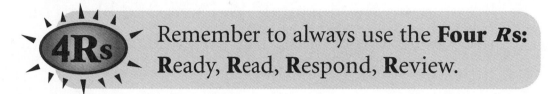

Remember to always use the **Four *Rs*: R**eady, **R**ead, **R**espond, **R**eview.

Multiple-Choice Questions

Remember to mark the best answer. If you are not sure of an answer, make the best guess you can. Then, go to the next question. You can check your answers later if you have time.

Short-Answer Questions

Write your answer on the line. You will write a few words as an answer.

Essay Questions

Graphic organizers help you answer essay questions. Fill in a graphic organizer. Use the graphic organizer to answer the essay question. After you finish writing, review your work. Use the checklist on page 110 to help you.

Welcome Home

"I would like to get Grandma a present when she gets home from the hospital," Wei said. "I'd like to buy her flowers or a new dress. But I don't have any money." Li didn't have money either.

"I have an <u>idea</u>," said Li. Li pulled a big box out of the closet. "Maybe we can make something for Grandma." In the box were ribbons, bows, and wrapping paper.

"I don't think we can make anything with this," said Wei. "Let's make a list of what Grandma likes." The girls made the list. Then they looked at each other and smiled. They had the perfect gift for Grandma.

The next day Grandma came home. Li and Wei ran over and kissed her. Both girls hugged Grandma and smiled at her.

"Thank you, girls," Grandma said. "You knew what I wanted—kisses, hugs, and smiles! It is so good to be home!"

DIRECTIONS: Read each question carefully. Fill in the bubble next to the best answer or write your answer on the lines.

1   How are Li and Wei related?

    Ⓐ They are cousins.

    Ⓑ They are sisters.

    Ⓒ They are grandmothers.

2   Another word for <u>idea</u> is

    Ⓐ present.

    Ⓑ thing.

    Ⓒ thought.

3   Where does this story take place?

    Ⓐ At a hospital

    Ⓑ In a house

    Ⓒ In a flower shop

4   Why didn't the girls buy Grandma flowers?

    Ⓐ Grandma doesn't like flowers.

    Ⓑ They didn't have any money.

    Ⓒ They wanted to buy a new dress.

5   What are the three gifts the girls gave to
their grandma?

_____

_____

_____

_____

Essay Question: Explain what happens in the story.

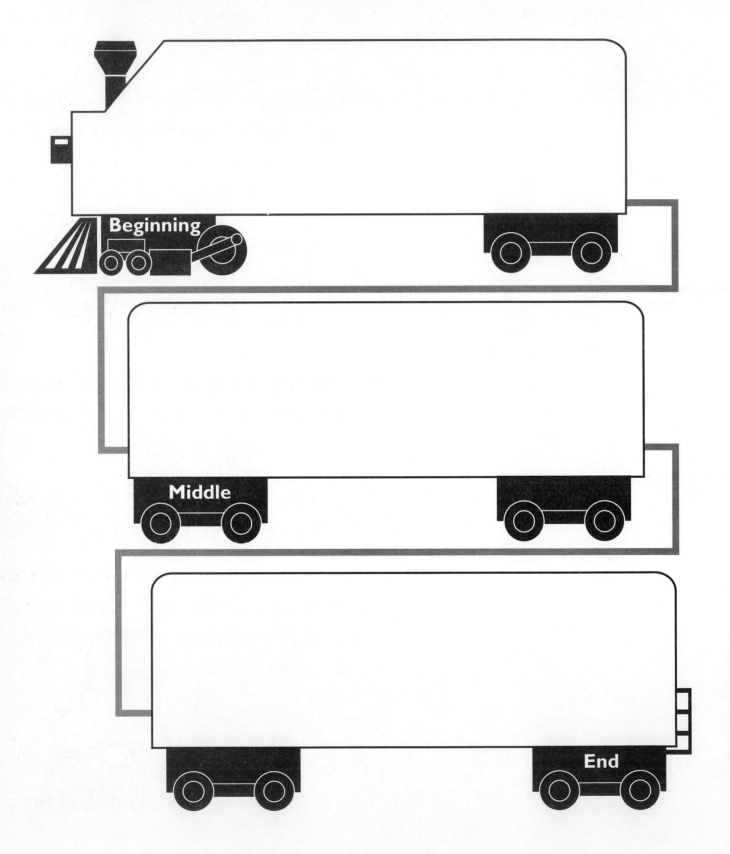

Follow the steps below. Then use the **Story Train** to answer the essay question. Write your answer on a separate sheet of paper.

1. Write what happens first in the story in the train engine.

2. Write what happens next in the middle car.

3. Write what happens last in the caboose.

6   Explain what happens in the story.

DIRECTIONS: Read this story about swallows and their flight to a special place each year. Then answer questions 7 through 12.

They Return Each Year

Do you know where you'll be on March 19? If you were a swallow, you'd know. Every year, the little birds return to a small town in California. This town is called San Juan Capistrano.

Swallows spend the winter in another country called Argentina. Then, the birds fly back to California. Their trip is very long!

At dawn, the first swallows appear in the sky. The people of the town ring church bells. This tells that the swallows have returned. Each year the birds build nests. The nests are made of mud. They are in the walls of an old church.

The <u>townspeople</u> celebrate the return of the birds. Visitors come from all over the world. You may not know where you'll be on March 19. But if you were in San Juan Capistrano, you know what you'd see.

DIRECTIONS: Read each question carefully. Fill in the bubble next to the best answer or write your answer on the lines.

7 Why do visitors go to San Juan Capistrano on March 19?

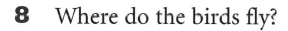

Ⓐ They want to see the swallows return.

Ⓑ They like to visit old churches.

Ⓒ It is a national holiday.

8 Where do the birds fly?

Ⓐ From all over the world to San Juan Capistrano

Ⓑ From Argentina to California

Ⓒ From an old church to San Juan Capistrano

9 Why did the author write this story?

Ⓐ To teach about a special event

Ⓑ To explain how birds fly

Ⓒ To tell a funny story

10 What does the word <u>townspeople</u> mean in the story?

Ⓐ A town with no people

Ⓑ The people who live in a town

Ⓒ The people who visit a town

I I   What do swallows use to build their nests?

_____

_____

_____

_____

Essay Question: Write a letter to your friend. Describe the swallows you just read about.

Follow the steps below. Then use the **Character Web** to answer the essay question. Write your answer on a separate sheet of paper.

1. Write what you want to describe in the middle cloud.

2. Read the story carefully. Look for words that describe what you wrote in the middle cloud.

3. Write these descriptive words in the smaller clouds around the middle cloud.

12 Write a letter to your friend. Describe the swallows you just read about.

DIRECTIONS: Read this story about two brothers who are very different. Then answer questions 13 through 21.

The Walker Brothers Wear Hats

The Walker brothers were different. William was serious. Jason was silly. But both were excited about Friday. It was Hat Day at Park Side School. William wanted to win the prize for Best Hat From History. This prize goes to the hat that comes from a time long ago. Jason hoped to win the Funniest Hat prize. This prize goes to the silliest hat.

On Monday, William and Jason started making their hats. Jason cut green cloth into scales. He glued them onto a cap. William looked at a picture of Abraham Lincoln. He took black paper and rolled it into a tall hat like the one Lincoln wore. The boys worked every night after that.

Finally, Hat Day arrived. William got up early. He took a long shower. He put on a white T-shirt and black pants. Jason slept late. Mom had to shake him twice. The first time he didn't wake up. Jason took a quick bath. Then he put on a green T-shirt and shorts.

Mom took a picture of the boys in their hats. William wore his tall black hat. Jason's hat looked like a dinosaur head. Mom said, "You both worked very hard on your hats. I hope you have fun at school today."

After lunch, the children put on their hats. Each class paraded through the library.

Finally, Ms. Wolfe named the winners. "The Funniest Hat prize goes to William Walker! We think his tall hat is so silly!" William's eyes grew wide. He walked up front and got his ribbon.

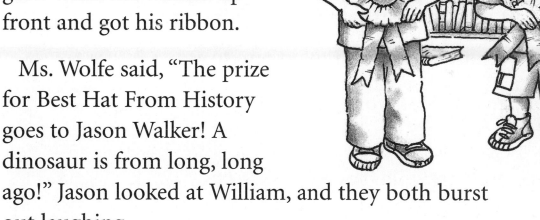

Ms. Wolfe said, "The prize for Best Hat From History goes to Jason Walker! A dinosaur is from long, long ago!" Jason looked at William, and they both burst out laughing.

"Wait until Mom hears about this!" they both said.

DIRECTIONS: Read each question carefully. Fill in the bubble next to the best answer or write your answer on the lines.

13 You can tell that the brothers' mom is

Ⓐ not interested in what they do.

Ⓑ tired from helping them make their hats.

Ⓒ very proud of both of her sons.

14 The boys made hats

Ⓐ to wear at their school Hat Day.

Ⓑ because their mom told them to.

Ⓒ because Ms. Wolfe likes hats.

15 To make a hat like Lincoln's, William

     (A) glued green cloth to a cap.

     (B) looked at a picture of
Abraham Lincoln.

     (C) asked Jason for help.

16 Why did the brothers laugh at the end of the story?

     (A) They were happy that Hat Day was over.

     (B) They each won the prize that the other
brother wanted.

     (C) They thought that their hats were funny-looking.

17 The author wrote the story to

Ⓐ tell a funny story.

Ⓑ tell how to make hats.

Ⓒ tell about contests.

18 What do you think William and Jason will do next?

Ⓐ They will wear each other's hats.

Ⓑ They will make new hats.

Ⓒ They will tell their mother about the contest.

19 What day of the week is Hat Day?

_____

_____

20 What do the children do on Hat Day at Park
Side School?

_____

_____

_____

_____

Essay Question: The story says that the Walker brothers are different. How are the two boys ALIKE?

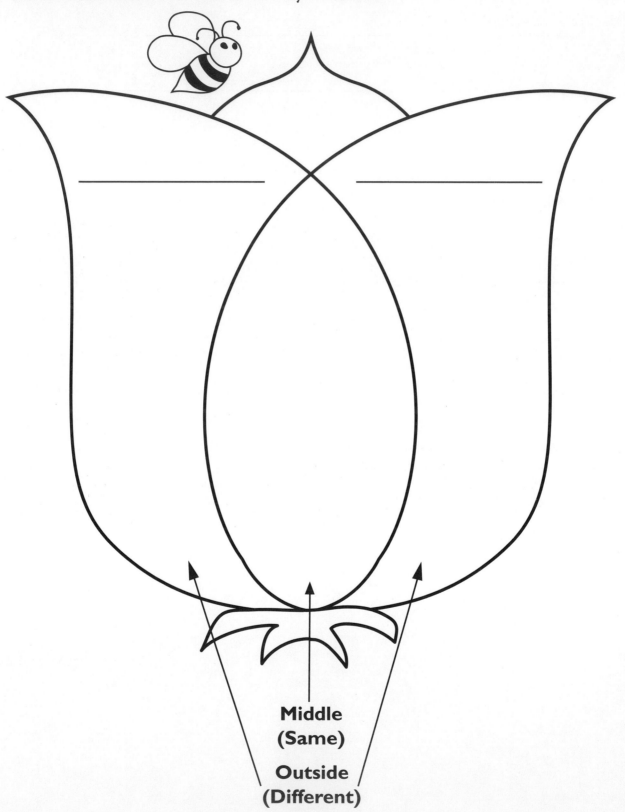

**Middle
(Same)**

**Outside
(Different)**

Follow the steps below. Then use the **Venn Diagram** to answer the essay question. Write your answer on a separate sheet of paper.

> **1.** Fill in the lines at the top of the flower with the two things you want to compare.
>
> **2.** Reread the story to find how the two boys are different. Write how they are different in the **outside** part.
>
> **3.** Look at the story to find how the two boys are alike. Write how they are alike in the **middle** part.

21 The story says that the Walker brothers are different. How are the two boys ALIKE?

DIRECTIONS: Read this poem about a girl with a new umbrella. Then answer questions 22 through 27.

Bella Had a New Umbrella

by Eve Merriam

1 Bella had a new umbrella,

2 Didn't want to lose it,

3 So when she walked out in the rain

4 She didn't ever use it.

5 Her nose went sniff,

6 Her shoes went <u>squish</u>,

7 Her socks grew soggy,

8 Her glasses got foggy,

9 Her pockets filled with water

10 And a little green froggy.

11 All she could speak was a weak *kachoo*!

12 But Bella's umbrella

13 Stayed nice and new.

DIRECTIONS: Read each question carefully. Fill in the bubble next to the best answer or write your answer on the lines.

22 Read these lines from the poem.

> **7 Her socks grew soggy,**
>
> **8 Her glasses got foggy,**
>
> **9 Her pockets filled with water**
>
> **10 And a little green froggy.**

Which lines rhyme?

Ⓐ 7 and 8 only

Ⓑ 9 and 10

Ⓒ 7, 8, and 10

23 Why do Bella's pockets fill with water?

Ⓐ She left her raincoat in the rain.

Ⓑ She does not use her umbrella in the rain.

Ⓒ She wants a frog to live there.

24 Bella does not use her umbrella because

   Ⓐ she doesn't want to lose it.

   Ⓑ she forgot it.

   Ⓒ she lost it.

25 In line 6, what does the word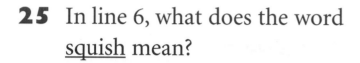
<u>squish</u> mean?

   Ⓐ A loud, banging sound

   Ⓑ A talking sound

   Ⓒ A splashing sound when walked on

26 What two things were in Bella's pockets?

_____

_____

_____

_____

Essay Question: How did Bella feel at the end of her walk? Use details from the poem in your answer.

Follow the steps below. Then use the **Character Web** to answer the essay question. Write your answer on a separate sheet of paper.

1. Write what you want to describe in the middle cloud.

2. Reread the poem. Look for words that describe what you wrote in the middle cloud.

3. Write these descriptive words in the smaller clouds around the middle cloud.

27 How did Bella feel at the end of her walk? Use details from the poem in your answer.

DIRECTIONS: First read the story about the wish of a princess. Then answer questions 28 through 36.

The Dancing Princess

Once upon a time, a king said to his daughter, "What would you like? Would you like a new comb or a new brush? Would you like a horse to ride?"

The princess said, "Father, I would like to be the <u>best</u> dancer in the kingdom!" The king found the best dance teacher in the kingdom. He hired <u>musicians</u> to play dance music.

The dance teacher helped the princess move her feet. But the princess fell down. He helped her move her arms. But she broke two lamps. The princess wanted more. She said, "Father, I want to be the best dancer in the kingdom!"

The king went to the shoemaker. "Shoemaker, the princess wants to dance. Make her the finest dancing slippers in the kingdom."

This page may not be reproduced without permission of Steck-Vaughn/Berrent.

The next day, the shoemaker brought a pair of beautiful magic shoes to the castle. He put them on the princess's feet. Then, the shoemaker said, "Dance!"

The band began to play. The princess twirled. She leaped. She moved smoothly across the dance floor. The music stopped. But the princess kept on dancing!

She danced to dinner that night. "Father," she said. "At first, I was not a good dancer." She twirled and leaped as she ate her dinner. "I am now a good dancer. But I cannot stop. I am not happy. Help me have fun again!"

The king danced the princess to the dance hall. He told the band to play some music. Soon the princess was leaping and hopping. She leaped over the king. He grabbed one shoe and pulled it off. She leaped again. He pulled off the other shoe. The princess tripped and sat on the floor.

"Thank you," the princess said. "From now on, I will dance to enjoy the music. It doesn't matter if I am good or not. I just want to be happy!"

DIRECTIONS: Read each question carefully. Fill in the bubble next to the best answer or write your answer on the lines.

28 What caused the princess to dance well?

   Ⓐ The dance hall

   Ⓑ The fairy godmother

   Ⓒ The magic shoes

29 What might the princess do next?

   Ⓐ She will put the magic shoes on and dance at school.

   Ⓑ She will dance for fun without the magic shoes.

   Ⓒ She will dance in her new dress.

30 The boxes show some things that happened in the story.

1	2	3
The princess took dance lessons.		The princess couldn't stop dancing.

Which event belongs in Box 2?

Ⓐ The princess put on the magic shoes.

Ⓑ The king took the shoes off the princess's feet.

Ⓒ The king asked the princess what she wanted.

31 You can tell that the word <u>musicians</u> means

Ⓐ people who dance.

Ⓑ people who play music.

Ⓒ people who play games.

32 The princess says "Father, I would like to be the <u>best</u> dancer in the kingdom!" What word means the OPPOSITE of <u>best</u>?

Ⓐ greatest

Ⓑ oldest

Ⓒ worst

33 How did the king help the princess?

Ⓐ He taught her how to dance.

Ⓑ He took the magic shoes off her feet.

Ⓒ He fed her dinner.

34 What happened when the dance teacher showed the princess how to move her arms?

_____

_____

_____

35 Who makes the magic shoes for the princess?

_____

_____

Essay Question: What lesson did the princess learn at the end of the story?

Beginning

Middle

End

Follow the steps below. Then use the **Story Train** to answer the essay question. Write your answer on a separate sheet of paper.

> **1.** Write what happens first in the story in the train engine.
>
> **2.** Write what happens next in the middle car.
>
> **3.** Write what happens last in the caboose.

36 What lesson did the princess learn at the end of the story?

☑ Check Your Writing

☐ Did you answer the question completely?

☐ Did you explain what you are writing about in the first sentence?

☐ Do all of your words make sense?

☐ Did you capitalize the first word of every sentence?

☐ Did you end every sentence with the correct punctuation mark?

☐ Is everything spelled correctly?

☐ Is your handwriting neat?

Answer Sheet

STUDENT'S NAME																			SCHOOL:
LAST									FIRST									MI	TEACHER:

FEMALE ○   MALE ○

BIRTH DATE

MONTH	DAY		YEAR	
Jan ○	⓪	⓪	⑦	⓪
Feb ○	①	①	⑧	①
Mar ○	②	②	⑨	②
Apr ○	③	③	⓪	③
May ○		④		④
Jun ○		⑤		⑤
Jul ○		⑥		⑥
Aug ○		⑦		⑦
Sep ○		⑧		⑧
Oct ○		⑨		⑨
Nov ○				
Dec ○				

GRADE ① ② ③ ④ ⑤

Reading & Writing Excellence Level B

Name/grid columns: A B C D E F G H I J K L M N O P Q R S T U V W X Y Z (repeated per column)

TEST

1 Ⓐ Ⓑ Ⓒ	10 Ⓐ Ⓑ Ⓒ	19 short-answer	28 Ⓐ Ⓑ Ⓒ
2 Ⓐ Ⓑ Ⓒ	11 short-answer	20 short-answer	29 Ⓐ Ⓑ Ⓒ
3 Ⓐ Ⓑ Ⓒ	12 essay	21 essay	30 Ⓐ Ⓑ Ⓒ
4 Ⓐ Ⓑ Ⓒ	13 Ⓐ Ⓑ Ⓒ	22 Ⓐ Ⓑ Ⓒ	31 Ⓐ Ⓑ Ⓒ
5 short-answer	14 Ⓐ Ⓑ Ⓒ	23 Ⓐ Ⓑ Ⓒ	32 Ⓐ Ⓑ Ⓒ
6 essay	15 Ⓐ Ⓑ Ⓒ	24 Ⓐ Ⓑ Ⓒ	33 Ⓐ Ⓑ Ⓒ
7 Ⓐ Ⓑ Ⓒ	16 Ⓐ Ⓑ Ⓒ	25 Ⓐ Ⓑ Ⓒ	34 short-answer
8 Ⓐ Ⓑ Ⓒ	17 Ⓐ Ⓑ Ⓒ	26 short-answer	35 short-answer
9 Ⓐ Ⓑ Ⓒ	18 Ⓐ Ⓑ Ⓒ	27 essay	36 essay